COACHING KIDS SOCCER

AGES 5 TO 10

VOLUME 1

This book is for first time coaches, volunteers, parents and anyone wanting to coach!

Set up simple, fun and effective drills and organise a training session in 5 minutes!

CHRIS KING

COACHING KIDS SOCCER - AGES 5 TO 10 - VOLUME 1

This book is for first time coaches, volunteers & any would be coach.

Set up simple, fun and effective drills & organise a practice session in 5 minutes!

This short book is intended for people coaching kids the basics of soccer aged between 5 to 10. It's a great starting point as the drills are designed to be easy to set up and run, as well as being flexible to adapt to different numbers of kids and skill levels.

Don't think too much about being an expert coach - your main job is to encourage and help the children enjoy themselves. All the drills in this book will show you how to run a fun and successful practice session.

The most effective way to get young children to learn soccer is to just let them play for the majority of the time through a game & fun drills.

This book includes instructions and images of how to run practice sessions and includes different drills and games for each of the main parts of a practice session. Enjoy!

Chris King

Chris King

OTHER SOCCER COACHING BOOKS BY CHRIS KING:

Training Sessions For Soccer Coaches Volume 1

Training Sessions For Soccer Coaches Volume 2

Training Sessions For Soccer Coaches Volume 3

Attacking & Shooting Drills For Soccer Coaches

Soccer Rondos Volume 1

Soccer Rondos Volume 2

Coaching Kids Soccer - Volume 1

Coaching Kids Soccer - Volume 2

Coaching Kids Soccer - Volume 3

The Ultimate Soccer Coaching Bundle Volume 1

110 Drills For Soccer Coaches

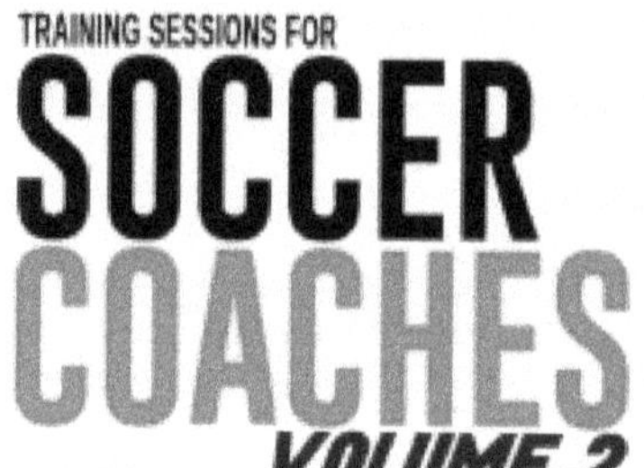

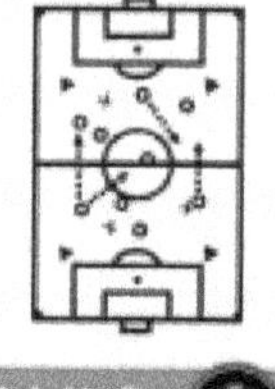

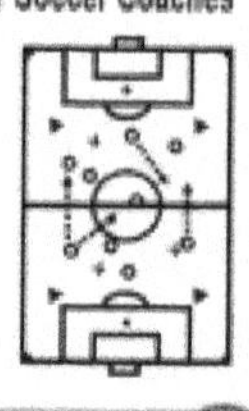

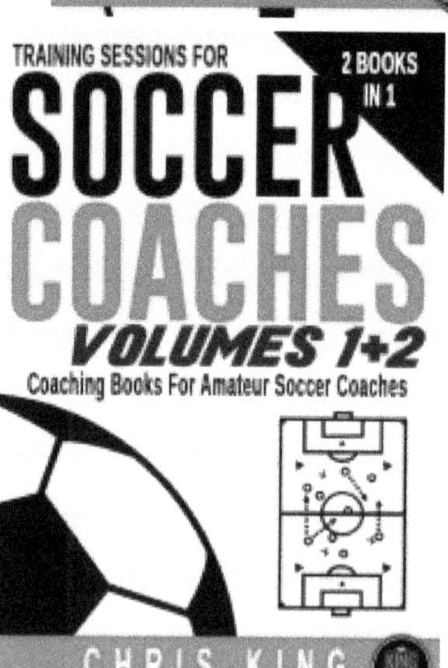
TRAINING SESSIONS FOR
SOCCER
2 BOOKS
IN 1
COACHES
VOLUMES 1+2
Coaching Books For Amateur Soccer Coaches
CHRIS KING

SOCCER
RONDOS
VOLUME 1
Coaching Books For Amateur Soccer Coaches
SOCCER
RONDOS
VOLUME 2
Coaching Books For Amateur Soccer Coaches

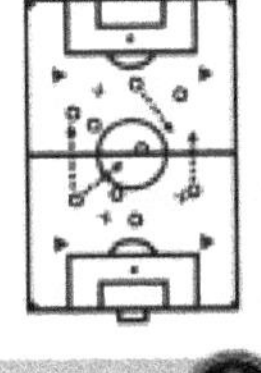

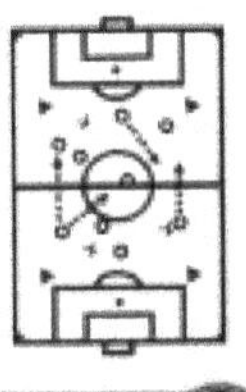

CHRIS KING
CHRIS KING

2 BOOKS
IN 1
SOCCER
RONDOS
VOLUMES 1+2
Coaching Books For Amateur Soccer Coaches
CHRIS KING

COACHING KIDS SOCCER
AGES 5 TO 10
VOLUME 1
This book is for first time coaches, volunteers, parents and anyone wanting to coach!
Set up simple, fun and effective drills and organise a training session in 5 minutes!
CHRIS KING
COACHING KIDS SOCCER
AGES 5 TO 10
VOLUME 2
This book is for first time coaches, grassroots coaches, volunteers and parents!
Set up simple soccer drills that teach kids skills while having fun!
CHRIS KING

COACHING KIDS SOCCER
AGES 5 TO 10
VOLUME 3
This book is for first time coaches, volunteers & any would be coach
Set up simple, fun and effective drills & organise a practice session in 5 minutes!
CHRIS KING
2 BOOKS IN 1
COACHING KIDS SOCCER
VOLUMES 1-2
This book is for first time coaches, volunteers & any would be coach
Set up simple fun and effective drills & organise a practice session in 5 minutes!
CHRIS KING

ATTACKING & SHOOTING DRILLS FOR
SOCCER
COACHES
VOLUME 1
Coaching Books For Amateur Soccer Coaches
CHRIS KING
5 BOOKS IN 1!
THE ULTIMATE
SOCCER
COACHING
BUNDLE
VOLUME ONE
CHRIS KING

7 BOOKS IN 1!
110
DRILLS FOR
SOCCER
COACHES
Coaching Books For Amateur Soccer Coaches
THIS BOOK INCLUDES 7 BOOKS IN 1!
CHRIS KING

© Copyright 2021 - CHRIS KING

TIPS ON WHAT TO DO BEFORE YOU START A PRACTICE SESSION

This is how I run my sessions for either a 30 or 60 minute session (allowing 5 to 10 minutes for explaining drills & packing up).

- 30 minute session is broken down into 5 minutes for each part
- 60 minute session is broken down into 10 minutes for each part

Each training session is broken down into 5 parts:

1. SMALL SIDED GAME - 5 or 10 mins

2. FUN GAME - 5 or 10 mins

3. SMALL SIDED GAME (WITH A SLIGHT CHANGE) - 5 or 10 mins

4. SKILLS & MOVEMENT - 5 or 10 mins

5. SMALL SIDED GAME - 5 or 10 mins

SESSION LAYOUT

1. SMALL SIDED GAME	2. FUN GAME	3. SMALL SIDED GAME (WITH A SLIGHT CHANGE)	4. SKILLS & MOVEMENT	5. SMALL SIDED GAME
5 - 10 MINUTES	5 - 10 MINUTES	5 - 10 MINUTES	5 - 10 MINUTES	5 - 10 MINUTES
4V4 OR 5V5 ON A SMALL PITCH WITH GOALS.	FUN GAMES RELATED TO FOOTBALL. AN OPPORTUNITY FOR EACH CHILD TO EXPERIENCE SUCCESS & SPEND TIME ON THE BALL. USE GAMES SUCH AS "GATES" "END ZONE".	4V4 OR 5V5 ON A SMALL PITCH WITH GOALS. INTRODUCE A SCORING SYSTEM TO ENCOURAGE CERTAIN SKILLS.	DEVELOP CHILDRENS BASIC SKILLS & MOVEMENT TO GIVE THEM CONFIDENCE. USE GAMES SUCH AS "KNOCK IT OFF" "SIMON SAYS".	4V4 OR 5V5 ON A SMALL PITCH WITH GOALS.

The main thing with this training session is that you should start and finish with a Small Sided Game (parts 1 & 5). Only parts 2 & 4 change & part 3 has a slight change.

In this book I will show you how to set up the small sided games in parts 1 & 5 and will give you 5 variations of part 2 (Fun Game) & part 4

(Skills & Movements) plus the variations for part 3 (Small Sided Game with a Slight Change).

Before getting into the sessions, here are a few things to keep in mind when training young children:

- You will have different levels of skill & experience so make sure to **encourage & praise all the players** - not just the ones that are at a better skill level

- Create opportunities where **all the children can experience success**

- **Be patient** & give them time to grasp what you are showing them

- Use games that encourage **every child to have a ball at their feet as much as possible**

- **Praise each child for their effort** no matter what the end result

- **Keep the children excited!** Act like an idiot or be over enthusiastic if you need to be

- **Use simple language** to explain & make sure to demonstrate

- **Encourage players to be creative**

- **Keep it fun** so they will want to come back next time

PRE-PRACTICE TIPS

- Arrive early so the activities are set up

- When the children start arriving, organise them into a game straight away

EQUIPMENT NEEDED

- 1 ball per child
- 12 cones
- 2 or 4 mini goals (use poles or cones if no goals)
- 4 sets of different coloured bibs

SETTING UP

If you're not sure exactly how many children you will have for the session, it's best to set up an extra mirror drill (two of the same drill) just in case. I like to set the two areas up side by side with a channel in the middle where I can see both areas and therefore keep an eye on everything plus I can distribute balls to both areas. (You can lose children's attention very quickly, so by having everything set up as much as possible ahead of time it leads to a smoothly run session).

Use the same coloured cone for one pitch and a different set of coloured cones for the other so it is clear to the children which pitch is which. (Then, for example, you can say to them "Team 1 and 2 on the pitch with yellow cones" & they know where to go straight away).

See the images below for how I set up (this example has 16 children with two 4v4 games) & then we'll get straight into the sessions.

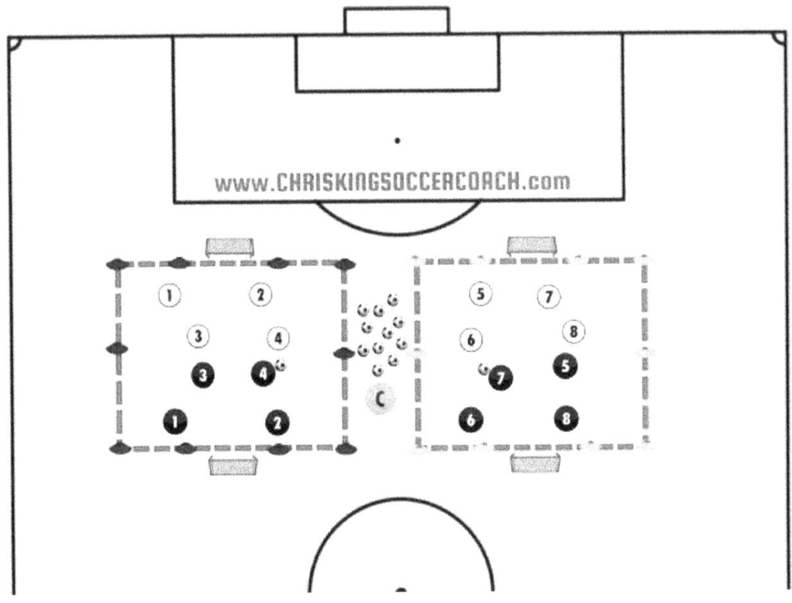

SESSION LAYOUT

Remember this is the order of the session:

1. SMALL SIDED GAME

2. FUN GAME

3. SMALL SIDED GAME (WITH A SLIGHT CHANGE)

4. SKILLS & MOVEMENT

5. SMALL SIDED GAME

SESSION LAYOUT

1. SMALL SIDED GAME	2. FUN GAME	3. SMALL SIDED GAME (WITH A SLIGHT CHANGE)	4. SKILLS & MOVEMENT	5. SMALL SIDED GAME
5 - 10 MINUTES	5 - 10 MINUTES	5 - 10 MINUTES	5 - 10 MINUTES	5 - 10 MINUTES
4V4 OR 5V5 ON A SMALL PITCH WITH GOALS.	FUN GAMES RELATED TO FOOTBALL. AN OPPORTUNITY FOR EACH CHILD TO EXPERIENCE SUCCESS & SPEND TIME ON THE BALL. USE GAMES SUCH AS "GATES" "END ZONE".	4V4 OR 5V5 ON A SMALL PITCH WITH GOALS. INTRODUCE A SCORING SYSTEM TO ENCOURAGE CERTAIN SKILLS.	DEVELOP CHILDRENS BASIC SKILLS & MOVEMENT TO GIVE THEM CONFIDENCE. USE GAMES SUCH AS "KNOCK IT OFF" "SIMON SAYS".	4V4 OR 5V5 ON A SMALL PITCH WITH GOALS.

Okay let's get started on the first section....

1. SMALL SIDED GAME

This is a great way to start the session - simply get the children straight into a game!

- Mark out a small field (approx 20x15 metres for a 4v4/5v5 game).

- Organise the children into 2 teams & distribute bibs (try to keep it to 4 or 5 a side so that all the players are getting plenty of touches. If there are more than 8-10 players, set up another field)

- 1 point for a goal

Tell them if a ball goes out, leave it & you'll pass one in (this way they get the most amount of game time without having to chase a ball everytime it goes out. If you run out of balls stop for a minute & get the kids to run & grab them all for you. This saves time & also teaches them to help out).

Then give them 3 simple instructions & start the game:

- "No goalkeepers."

- "Don't use your hands."

- "Have fun!"

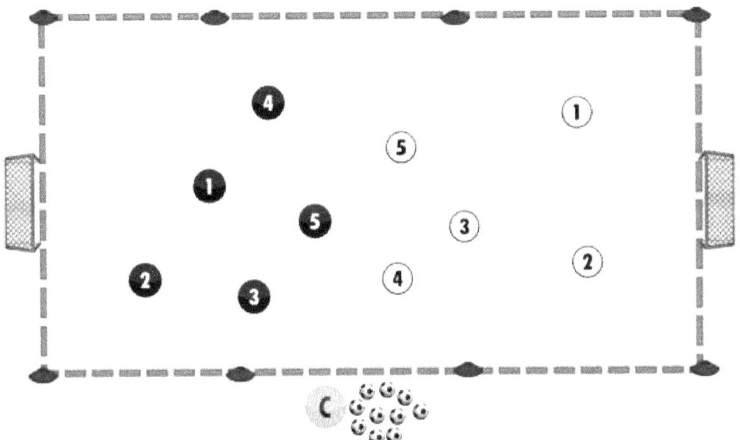
4
1
5
2
3
5
3
4
1
2
C

FUN GAME

This is a game related to football and is the chance to get all the children to experience success.

It should focus on a core skill such as running with the ball, passing, control or shooting.

Here are 5 different exercises to use for Section 2 of your sessions:

FUN GAME #1

"GATES"

• Set up 5 or 6 'gates' spread around the pitch by using two cones of the same colour.

• Players will dribble with the ball & run through the gates as many times in a certain period (30 seconds to 1 minute is ideal) & get one point for each gate they dribble through. They cannot run back through the same gate until they've been through a different one.

• After each period of time, ask the children how many gates they got through & then get them to beat that number in the next go.

• PROGRESSION: #1 -Make the gates smaller or larger depending on skill level. #2 - Partner the children up & get them to pass through the gates.

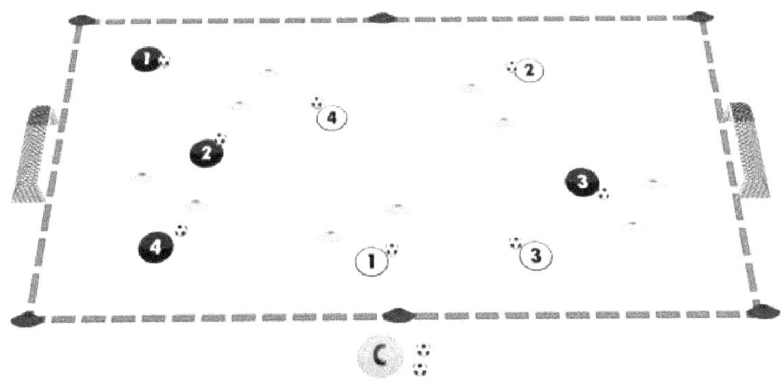

FUN GAME #2

"IT'S A KNOCK OFF"

- Split the children into 2 teams & place 3 balls on top of cones at each end.

- Similar to a regular game players have one ball but aim to knock the opposition's balls off with a pass instead of scoring in a goal. The first team to knock all 3 balls off wins.

- PROGRESSION: Make the pitch smaller or larger depending on skill level.

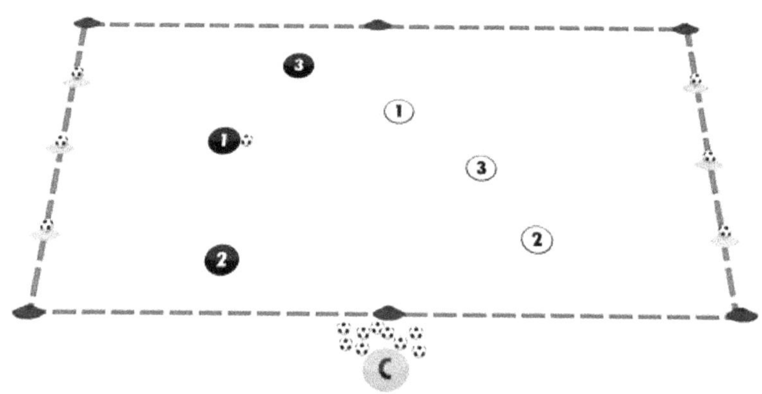

FUN GAME #3

"END ZONE"

- This is similar to the old game of British Bulldog.
- Split the children so there are two defenders without a ball at one end & the rest of the players with a ball at the other.
- Players with the ball try to get to the opposite end zone.
- The 2 defenders try to get a ball off the players & score at the end the players have just dribbled from. If successful in scoring they swap with the player they took the ball off.
- Once all the attackers have reached the opposite end zone, play restarts in the opposite direction when everyone is ready.
- PROGRESSION: Players use their non preferred foot.

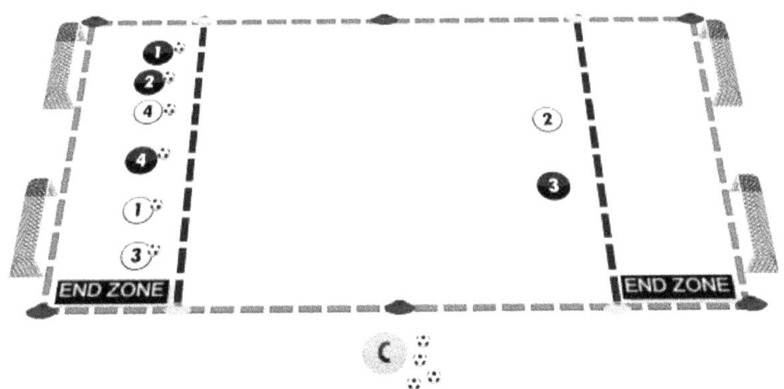

FUN GAME #4

“WORLD CUP”

- Set up 2 smaller areas with mini goals at each end.

- Split the players into teams of two (ie if 8 players there are 4 teams of 2).

- Teams play each other in 3 minute matches. Teams get 3 points for a win & 1 for a draw. Once they’ve played each other once, total up the points & the top 2 teams play off for the World Cup & bottom 2 play for 3rd place.

REVIEWS

"These books are great for new coaches.They have plenty of information and are easy to understand." Amazon review

"It teaches you how to set up training and be well organised in running coaching sessions!" Amazon review

ABOUT THE BOOK

Are you a first time coach, parent or volunteer new to coaching grassroots soccer and don't know where to start?

Or perhaps you just don't have the time to plan a training session?

In this book, I've put together tips and advice for new coaches plus FUN SKILL BASED GAMES THAT KIDS LOVE, **so you can be confident in taking a children's soccer training session without previous experience.**

These this easy to understand volume include drills for teaching soccer skills to children through FUN, EASY TO SET UP AND RUN GAMES. These books include:

- **Games and drills with diagrams throughout**
- **Tips on what to keep in mind when teaching young children**
- **How to easily plan and set up your training sessions in 5 minutes**

- **Heaps of fun and skill based games to keep the kids coming back ("Space Invaders", "Zombies", "Cops and Robbers" plus many more)!**

Available soccer coaching titles by Chris King:

Coaching Kids Soccer - Volume 1

Coaching Kids Soccer - Volume 2

Coaching Kids Soccer - Volume 3

Training Sessions For Soccer Coaches Volume 1

Training Sessions For Soccer Coaches Volume 2

Training Sessions For Soccer Coaches Volume 3

Attacking & Shooting Drills For Soccer Coaches

Soccer Rondos Volume 1

Soccer Rondos Volume 2

10 Soccer Drills - Volume 1

The Ultimate Soccer Coaching Bundle Volume 1

A bit about Chris...

Chris has played soccer since he was 5 (and still play socially in his late 40s as well as coaching).

He has completed coaching courses and coached men, women and children's teams. Chris has released 9 soccer coaching books on Amazon, all aimed at helping coaches improve themselves and their players. His partner also plays soccer, so they stay fit together.

- Have a fun penalty shoot out at the end.

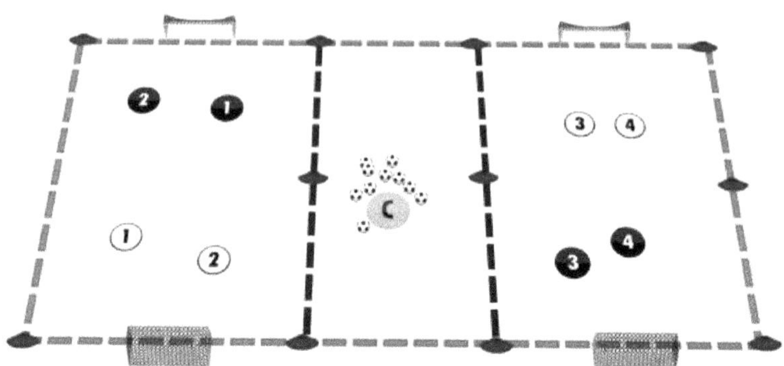
2
1
3
4
C
1
2
4
3

FUN GAME #5

"IT'S A RACE"

- Set up 2 goals with 4 balls in the middle. Split the children into two teams & number them off.

- The coach calls a number (ie "3!") and the two number 3's race to the middle. The player that gets the ball runs back & tries to score in the goal from the end they just ran from with the other player trying to stop them.

- First team to 5 points wins.

- **PROGRESSION:** Call out two numbers at once so two players work together.

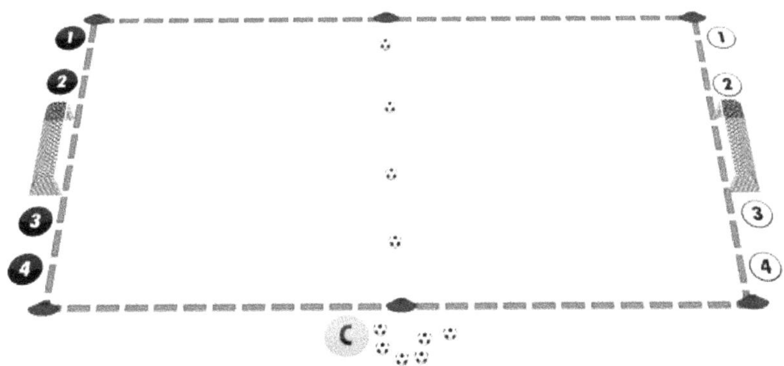

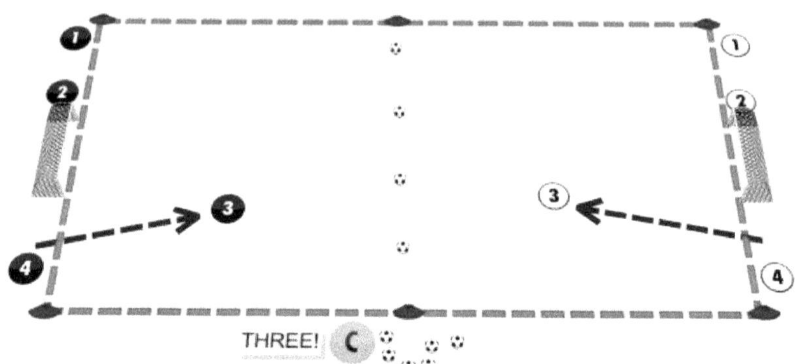
THREE!

SMALL SIDED GAME (WITH A SLIGHT CHANGE)

With this part, simply return to the original small sided game. But now add in a slight change to the rules so that you are encouraging the children to work on a skill for this session.

For example, if you are teaching the children to run with the ball, make a goal worth 2 points if they run past a player & score.

Introduce a scoring system to encourage certain skills & sportsmanship but it still stays as a regular, fun game.

Here are 5 changes to implement in different training sessions:

CHANGE 1: A goal is worth 2 points if a different player from the team scores the next goal.

CHANGE 2: A goal is worth 2 points if a player beats an opponent before scoring.

CHANGE 3: A goal is worth 2 points if a player scores with their non-prefered foot.

CHANGE 4: A player gets a high five if they stop a certain goal.

CHANGE 5: A player gets a high five if they help another player up off the ground.

SKILLS & MOVEMENT

This section focuses on developing children's basic skills & movement. These games/drills are easy to implement for all skill levels & aim at improving players general movement & giving them confidence. It is for any number of players plus they get to spend more time on the ball.

Here are 5 different exercises to use for section 4 of your sessions:

SKILLS & MOVEMENT GAME #1

"ROB THE NEST"

• Set up 4 goals (2 at each end) & 4 cones in the middle where all the footballs go.

• Split the players into 4 equal teams with each team starting in one of the corners.

• One player at a time from each group runs out & collects a ball from the centre, dribbles back & scores in their goal (as soon as the ball goes in the goal the next player can start).

• Play until there are no more balls in the centre & the team with the most goals at the end wins.

• **PROGRESSION:** Players can steal balls from other teams' goals once all balls from the centre are gone - play for a set time limit.

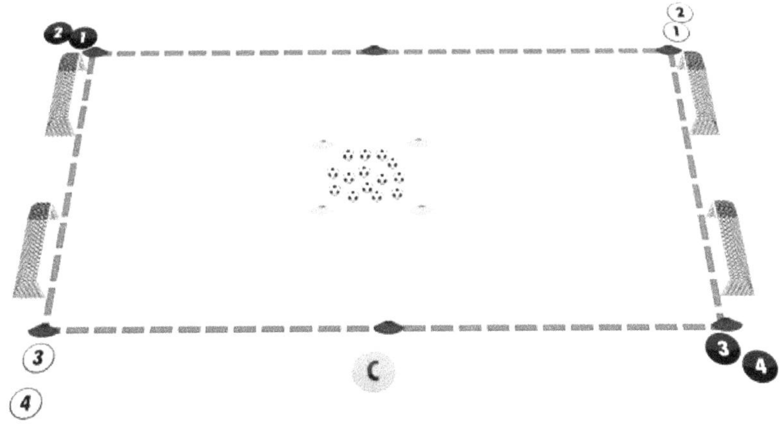

SKILLS & MOVEMENT GAME #2

"KNOCK IT OFF"

- Set up 4 cones in the middle with a ball on top of each cone.

- Players pair up with a ball per pair & start at either side of the cone.

- They attempt to kick the ball & knock off the ball in the middle in as few kicks as possible.

- Take note of how many passes it takes to knock the ball off (or how many times they knock it off) & then try to beat it on the next attempt.

- **PROGRESSION:** Change the distance the players are striking the ball from.

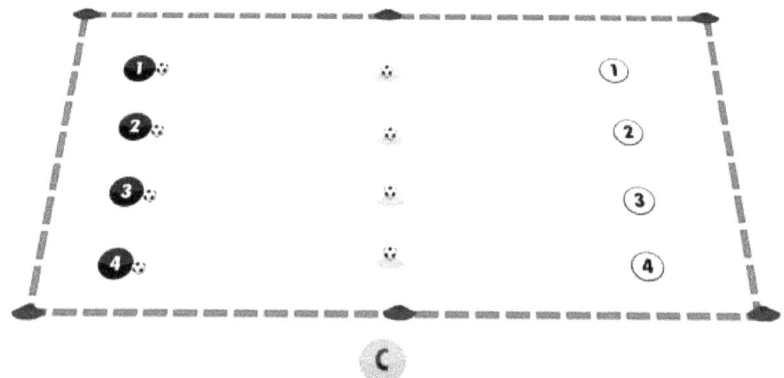

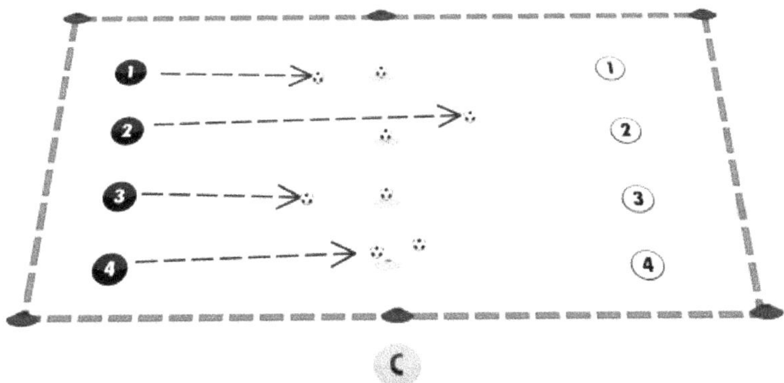
1
2
3
4
1
2
3
4
C

SKILLS & MOVEMENT GAME #3

"SIMON SAYS"

- Players dribble a ball inside an area.

- The coach will say "Simon Says..." followed by an instruction.

- Players do the instruction & then continue to dribble.

- Examples of some Simon Says instructions are: change direction; stop the ball; stop the ball & put your belly/knee/elbow on it; clap your hands between your legs; skip as you dribble; right foot only; stop your ball & find another; spell their name as they dribble.

- If the coach doesn't say "Simon Says" first & a player does the instruction have them do 10 toe taps on the ball.

- **PROGRESSION:** If a player gets caught out, issue them with a "Gotcha". The player/s with the least number of "Gotcha" at the end win.

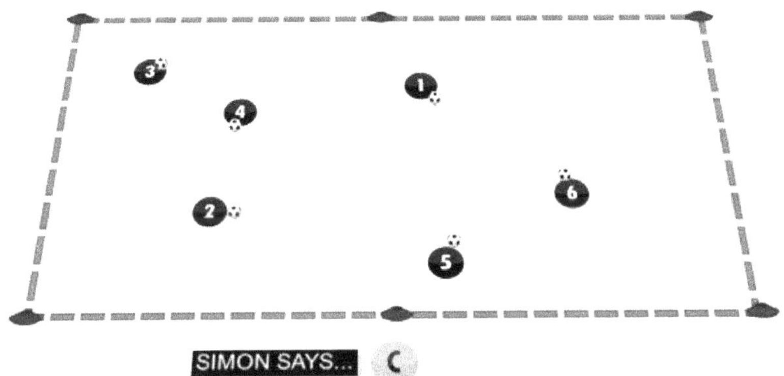
3
1
4
6
2
5
SIMON SAYS...

SKILLS & MOVEMENT GAME #4

"STUCK IN THE MUD"

• All players except for 2 have a ball & are dribbling around the designated area.

• The 2 players without balls run around & try & tag the other players. Once tagged players must pick their ball up with their hands & open their legs wide.

• Another player must pass their ball through that player's legs to release them & they are free to dribble again!

• Every one or two minutes change the tagging players.

• **PROGRESSION:** Have the players dribble with just their left/right foot.

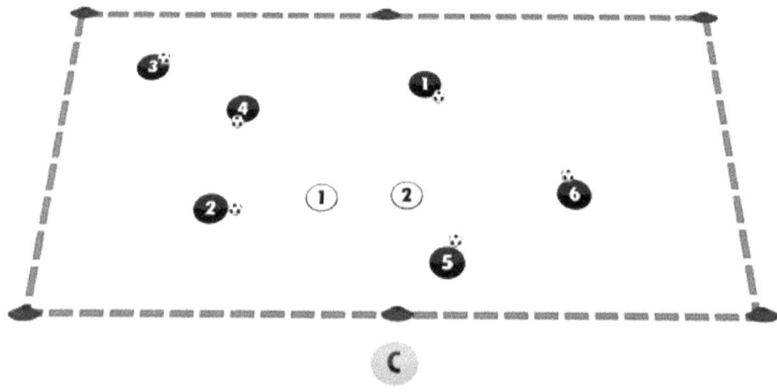

SKILLS & MOVEMENT GAME #5
"TRAFFIC LIGHTS"

- Set up two goals at one end & a starting line at the other end where all players line up with a ball. Players attempt to score a goal at the opposite end.

- The coach will call out "Green light!" which signals that the players can run with the ball & "Red light" which signals for players to stop.

- If the coach calls out "Red light" & a player doesn't stop or their ball is too far in front of them, they must return to the starting line.

- If a player scores a goal they get 1 point & return to the starting line.

- PROGRESSION: Call out driving instructions such as "Reverse" (go backwards for 5 yards). Also hold up a red or green bib or cone so players must look up to check on the instruction.

- Note: This drill can also be done without goals - simply have the players dribbling around in an area & "Green" means go faster, "Red" means stop, "Orange" means turn, etc.

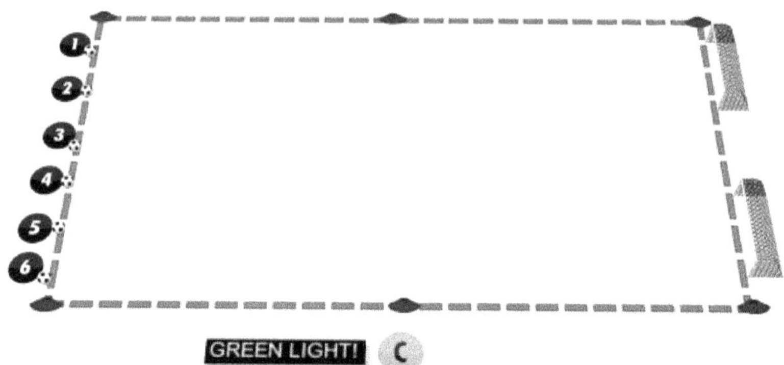
1
2
3
4
5
6
GREEN LIGHT!
C

SMALL SIDED GAME

This is the same as at the start. Let the kids finish with a game so they can enjoy themselves & try out anything new they've learnt from the session. Just sit back & encourage & praise aspects of their game. If you want to mix it up, feel free to put two goals at each end. This provides more scoring opportunities & therefore more opportunities for the children to experience success.

SUMMATION

The main focus for most players at this age is to make sure they have fun. If they do, they will keep coming back and will play at home as well.

Chris King

OTHER SOCCER COACHING BOOKS BY CHRIS KING

Coaching Kids Soccer Volume 2 now available!

COACHING KIDS SOCCER - AGES 5 TO 10 - VOLUME 2

Website: www.chriskingsoccercoach.com[1]

Facebook: www.facebook.com/chriskingsoccercoach[2]

1. http://www.chriskingsoccercoach.com

2. http://www.facebook.com/chriskingsoccercoach

COACHING KIDS SOCCER - VOLUME 2

This book is for coaches, volunteers, parents and anyone that wants to learn about coaching soccer.

I've done all the work for you! I've put together all the skills and games that you will need. In this book you will learn how to teach kids the essential skills they will need plus you will be able to set up simple, fun and effective games and drills.

So if you're ready to learn soccer games such as "Space Invaders", "Zombies" and "Shipwrecked With Sharks" let's get started!

Hello coaches and soccer fans!

Welcome to Volume 2 of Coaching Kids Soccer.

I had plenty of interest in the first volume so I decided there's definitely a need to continue to help with the coaching of our future soccer stars!

This book will be structured the same as the first one but it will be a lot longer. **I have included the key skills that kids need to learn early**

on to build a solid foundation for (hopefully) playing soccer their whole lives.

This book is intended for people who are coaching kids (approximately aged between 5 and 10) the basics of soccer.

It's a great starting point for coaches as the drills are designed to be easy to set up and run, as well as being **flexible to adapt to different numbers of kids and skill levels.**

Don't think too much about being an expert coach - your main job is to encourage and help the children enjoy themselves. **All the drills in this book will show you how to run a fun practice session.**

The most effective way to get young children to learn soccer is to let them play via games and fun drills.

This book **includes instructions and images** of how to run practice sessions and **includes different drills and games** for each of the main parts of a practice session.

Enjoy!

Chris King

Chris King

Drill from "Coaching Kids Soccer - Volume 2"

FUN GAME #2

"BARCELONA"◈

1. This game is all about passing and scoring but with a twist! It's very easy to set up and will help the kids with maths at the same time as having fun!

2. Set up a small field (20x30 yards) with small goals at each end.

3. Split the players into two teams (3v3 up to 5v5 works best) with no goalkeepers.

4. Regular soccer rules.

5. When a team has possession, count up the number of passes they make and if a goal is scored at the end, that team gets that amount of goals (ie if the team passes 8 times and scores they get 8 points! If they pass 3 times and score they get 3 points).

6. First team to 20 points wins.

7. Note: If the ball goes out take kick ins or the coach passes a new ball in.

WHAT TO FOCUS ON:

- Short passing and moving
- Good close ball control
- Move into space (can a player not on the ball lose their defender by doing a little shoulder drop and going in the other direction?)
- Work as a team

CHANGE IT:

Play 3 rounds of 2 minutes each and add up the total at the end instead of it being the first team to 20 points.

TIP:

Let the players play and just observe. Save the feedback until the end of a round.

PROGRESSION:

#1 Every player must touch the ball before a goal can be scored. This helps keep everyone involved plus you will see the talk improve and heads look around as the team communicates to make sure everyone has had a touch.

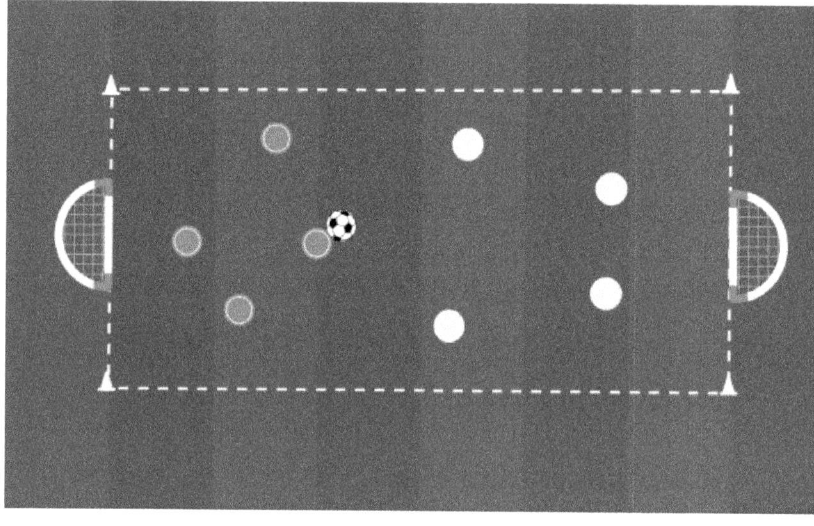

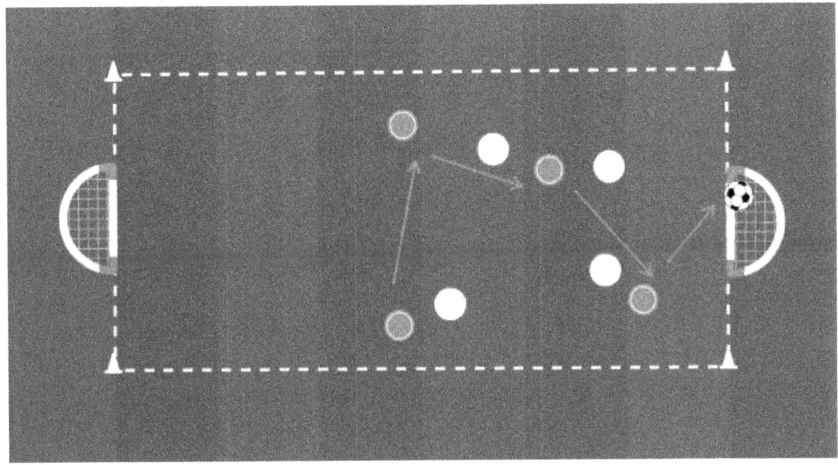

Summary of "Barcelona" :

- Regular soccer but with a scoring twist

- Each team passes until they score a goal. But make sure to count up the number of passes before the goal because the team gets this amount of points for the goal! (ie if they had 5 passes before scoring they get 5 points!)

- First team to 20 points wins

- In the above image the Red (dark) team have made 3 passes and then scored so they receive 3 points

---

Drills for "Coaching Kids Soccer - Volume 3"

GAME #7
"OUCH"

◈ FOCUS OF SESSION:

To encourage the kids to get their heads up while they dribble. This helps them to become aware of where the options are to pass and where the Defenders are.

This drill also helps with striking at a target.

◈ SET UP:

- **5 to 12 players + at least 1 Coach (or parent)!**
- 20x20 yard square

◈ THE DRILL:

What more can a player ask for than to get to kick a ball at the coach? In this game that's exactly what they get to do!

Each player starts inside the square with a ball and the coach starts inside the square without a ball.

When the coach says "Go!" players get to kick the ball at the coach - ***aiming for below the knees!*** This drill helps with the players being able to strike a ball on the move and also with scanning the area.

Each time the coach gets hit they should yell out "Ouch!" or something silly.

Play for 2 minutes, get the kids to keep count of how many times they have hit the coach and the player that has kicked their ball into the coach the most gets a high five from all the players.

◈ COACHES NOTES:

- Make sure to say that it has to be below the knee for it to count.

- The coach should change directions, dodge and weave so that the players have to look up to see where they are.

- Show the players the correct technique for passing/striking a ball: Eyes up to look at the target and then eyes back down on the ball to strike it. If it's a close range shot, it can be a pass with the instep. But if it's longer range, show them how to shoot with the laces to get more power.

☑ CHANGE IT:

- If the kids are struggling to hit the coach, slow down and stay in one spot for a second or two to make it easier for them.

- Can players use both feet to dribble and shoot?

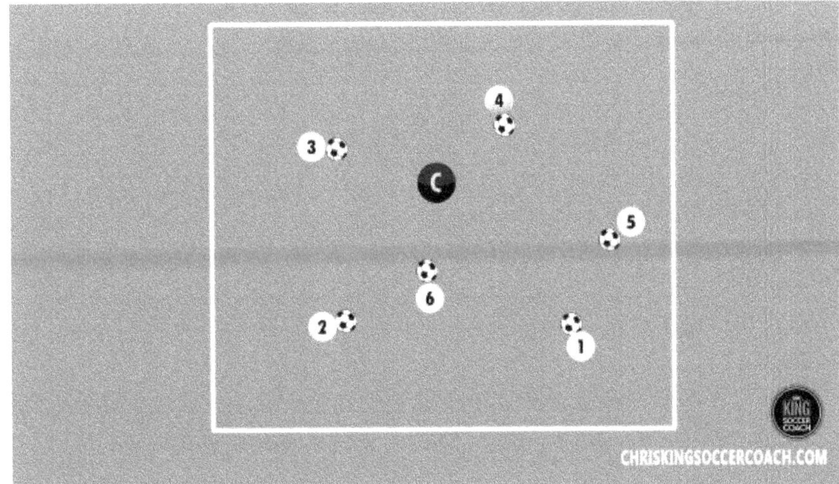

All the players start inside the square with a ball each. Once the coach says "Go!" the coach starts dodging around the square and the players get to pass/ strike the ball into the coach (below the knee!).

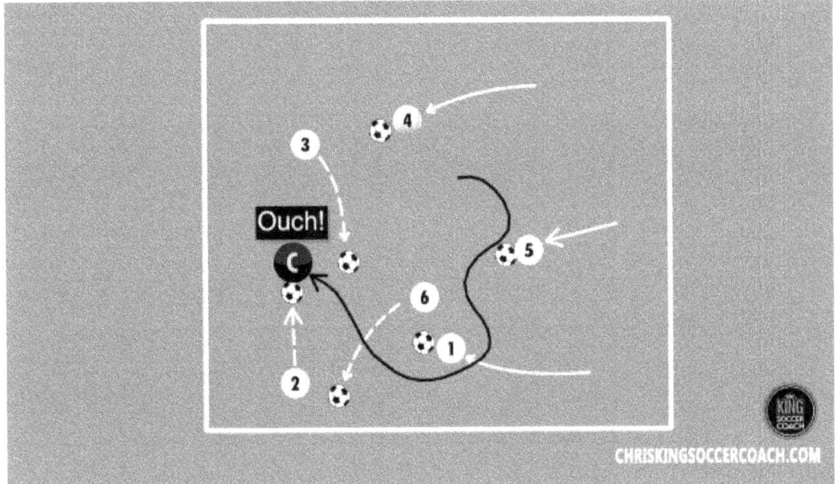

#6 and #3 missed the coach but #2's was a good strike and hit the coach below the knee!

GAME #8

"1v1"

◈ **FOCUS OF SESSION:**

Good ball control so as to be able to beat an opponent 1v1.

◈ **SET UP:**

- **6 to 10 players**
- 35x30 yard rectangle
- 6 mini goals

◈ **THE DRILL:**

Set up a large rectangle (approx 35x30 yards). Place 3 mini goals at each end.

Pair the players up, start at opposite ends with one player with a ball.

The Defender passes the ball to the Attacker who takes control and tries to beat the Defender and score in the goal closest to them at the other end.

If the Defender wins the ball they can try and score in the goal at the opposite end.

Swap roles after each turn.

Note: *Make sure to limit each go to approximately 10-20 seconds. We want to encourage the players to go at the Defender. Not stop, go back, shield the ball, etc.*

◈ COACHES NOTES:

- Make sure the players keep close control. They may want to dribble too fast but they need to keep it under control, otherwise it is easy for the Defender to win the ball. If they have lots of space in front of them they can take longer strides/ touches (i.e. have more than 1 step in between each touch). But when the Defender is closer they should be shorter touches (one step for every touch) so they can change direction easily and keep it away from the Defender.

- The Attacker should get their heads up as much as possible so they are away of where the Defender is. They should use different parts of the foot to change direction and get past the Defender.

- Different speeds can also help in getting past opponents. If they send the Defender one way with a feint, can they speed off the other direction?

☑ CHANGE IT:

- Team players up and play 2v2.

- Team all the players up into two teams and play against each other.

- If you don't have enough space or players are getting tired, have 2 pairs behind each other and take it in turns.

- Set up a cone for the players to practise against before moving on to a real 1v1 situation.

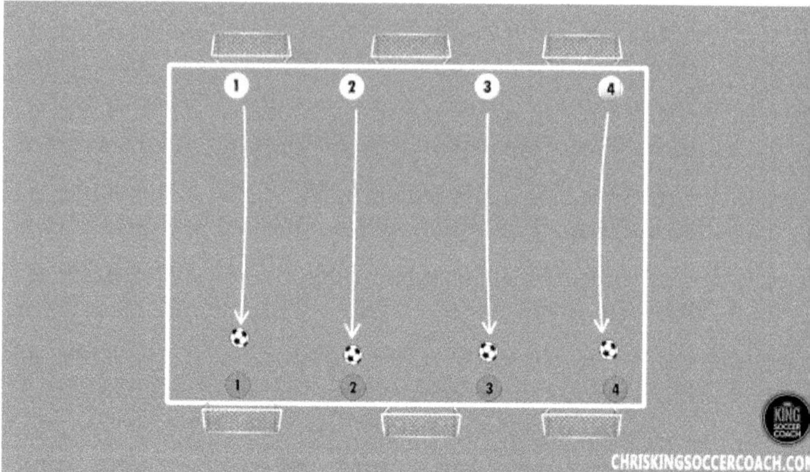

Players get to practise 1v1 situations. Defenders (Yellow) start with the ball and pass the ball to the Attackers to start play.

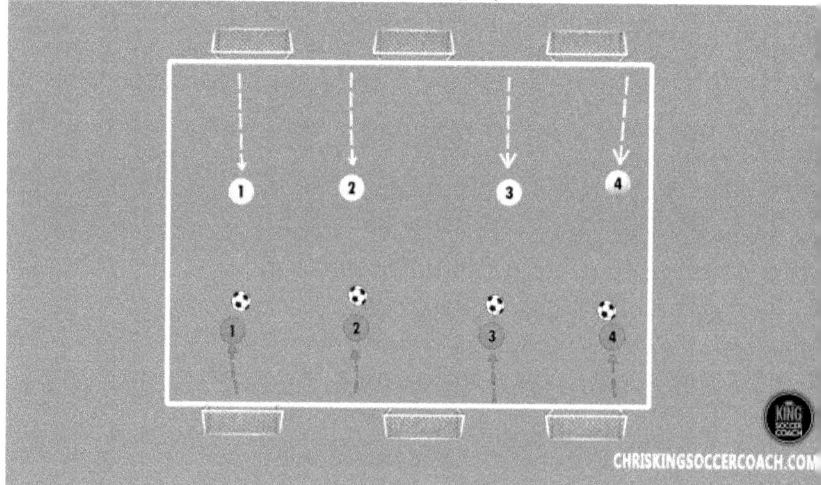

Defenders get out to the Attackers as fast as they can to shut them down. Attackers (Red) get to practise feints, shoulders drops, going at pace, etc to get past their Defender and score in the goal. Swap after each go.

GAME #9

"4 GOAL FUN SOCCER"

◈ FOCUS OF SESSION:

Let the kids learn by playing - just play soccer and have fun like they would at lunchtime at school. All skills will be worked on naturally.

◈ SET UP:

- **6 to 12 players**
- 35x25 yard rectangle
- 4 mini goals

◈ THE DRILL:

We want the kids to learn by doing, have success (i.e. score goals!) and not worry about any consequences of making mistakes. So let them play soccer and score lots of goals!

Set up a 35x25 yard rectangle with 4 goals (one on each side).

Split the players into 4 teams (ie if 8 players have 4 teams of 2. If you only have 6 players, have 3 teams of 2).

All teams play at once and can score in any goal!

As soon as a ball goes out or a goal is scored the coach should put another one in straight away. Also, sometimes put two balls at once! Twice the chaos, twice the fun and twice the goals.

The first team to 5 goals wins, then swap teams around.

◈ COACHES NOTES:

- Make sure everyone is having fun! Lots of encouragement and celebrating when goals are scored (high fives, rolly pollies, etc!).

- Encourage players to dribble, pass, take players on and shoot. This is a great chance for them to work out how to do things in a game situation.

☑ CHANGE IT:

#1 - Combine two teams (ie 4v4.). No need to even stop the game, just call out "Blues and greens are together versus yellow and reds."

#2 - Play 3 teams v 1. And if it's too hard for the 1 team, maybe the coach can join in and help them?

4 teams with 2 players each - players can score in any goal. This drill is all about having fun and scoring goals. Players get to practise all the skills they are learning (dribbling, passing, taking players on and shooting) in a fun environment.

GAME #10
"SURFERS AND SHARKS"

◈ FOCUS OF SESSION:

Dribbling and tackling (and passing when using the progression change).

◈ SET UP:

- **8 to 18 players**
- 35x25 rectangle with 3 different sized small squares inside the area

◈ THE DRILL:

Choose two players to be sharks who wait in the rectangle. The rest of the players are surfers and have a ball and start at one end.

Players practise their dribbling skills, aiming to surf (dribble) from one end of the ocean to the other without getting eaten (tackled) by a shark.

If a shark tackles a surfer and wins the ball they swap roles.

If the surfers need to, they can have a quick rest on one of the islands which are safe zones.

Once surfers reach the other end they turn around and come back. Who can get to the most ends?

Note: *Add or remove sharks if it's too easy or too hard for the surfers.*

◈ COACHES NOTES:

● Encourage players to use different parts of their feet when dribbling (inside and outside of both feet and soles).

● Use a change of speed (or direction!) to get past the sharks.

● Stop the ball on the islands (this will mean that players should have close control so they can stop it when required).

● Shield the ball when required. Can they keep the ball on the other side of the body so the shark can't tackle and steal the ball from them? Players should keep their arms/elbows up to help make them bigger and keep the sharks away from the ball.

● Sharks should look to win possession as soon as they can. If they've just become a shark, encourage them to keep their head up and win a ball back straight away. This helps in a real game situation as they won't give up if they lose a ball they will get in the habit to try and win back possession for their team straight away.

● Make sure surfers aren't spending too long on the islands. If they do bring in a 5-10 second limit.

☑ CHANGE IT:

#1 - Add players to the side and the surfers can do a one two pass with them to avoid being caught with the ball.

#2 - Add goals at each end. If surfers successfully make it from one end to the other they can have a shot at goal and receive a bonus point. Play for 5 minutes and see who gets the most points.

#3 - Team players up and see if they can pass their way through the ocean without being eaten by the sharks!

The two red sharks wait in the middle to see if they can catch a surfer and win the ball off them!

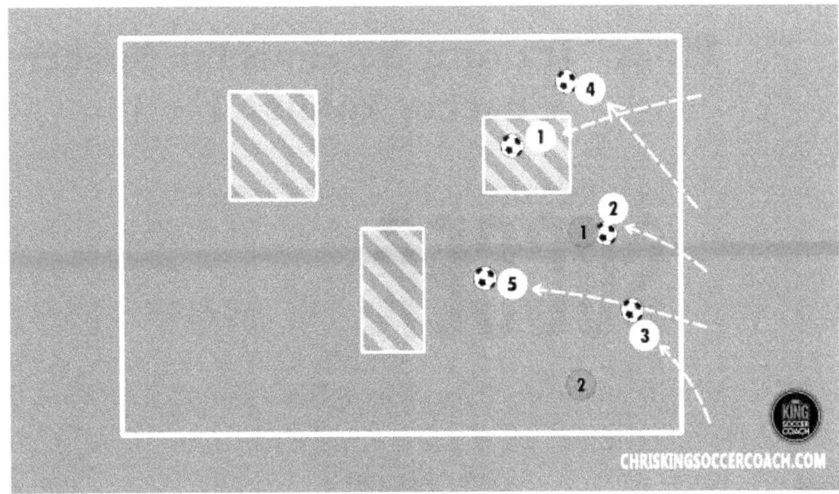

Yellow #4 is smart and goes wide away from the sharks. Yellow #1 goes straight for the first island and is safe and can plan their next move. Yellow #2 get eaten by a shark and must swap roles and become the shark.

From "Training Sessions For Soccer Coaches Volume 1"

CHAPTER 3

SESSION 1 - SUPPORTING THE ATTACK

Parts of the players game that will be improved from this session:

Supporting the attack; Pressing; Conditioning (fitness); Midfield players movement and awareness; Shooting.

SESSION 1 DRILL 1:

RONDO - PASSING & SHORT COMBINATION PLAY

PURPOSE:

- Improving passing in tight areas and improving the press.

SET UP:

- 10 Players (alternatively 6,8 or 12 players)
- 6 Cones
- 15 x 30 yards
- 15 Minutes

THE DRILL:

- Two teams of 5 players in each half.

- The ball begins with the Black team who attempt to pass and maintain possession.

- Once the first pass is made, one player from the White team (White #1 in this example) can press (creating a 5v1) and attempt to win the ball.

- Every 3 passes equal a goal and after each goal another player from the White team may enter to support the press (ie 5v2 once 3 passes [a goal] are made, 5v3 once 6 passes [2 goals] are made).

- If the White defenders win possession (or the ball goes out of play), they pass back into their waiting teammates in the opposite half and start passing and Black send a player in to create a 5v1.

KEY POINTS:

- Quality of the pass and make sure the attackers spread out.
- Split the defenders with the pass if possible.

- 1 or 2 touch maximum.

COACHES NOTES:

- Play can continue for 2 minutes and the team with the most goals wins, or alternatively the first team to 5 goals wins.

- Have spare balls spread around the outside for continuous, quick play.

- Tell defenders not to get split by a pass as this would take two players out of the action in a real game situation.

- Tell attackers to move the ball quickly, spread out, keep their heads up and split defenders where possible.

CHANGES/PROGRESSION:

- This drill works well with 3v3 and up to 6v6. Change the width of the field accordingly.

Starting Shape: 5v5. Black start in possession and as soon as Black #1 makes the first pass, a White (in this case White #1) runs into the other half to try and win possession. Once Black makes 3 passes another White can enter to help their team mate win possession and so on. (Image: Session 1 - drill 1)

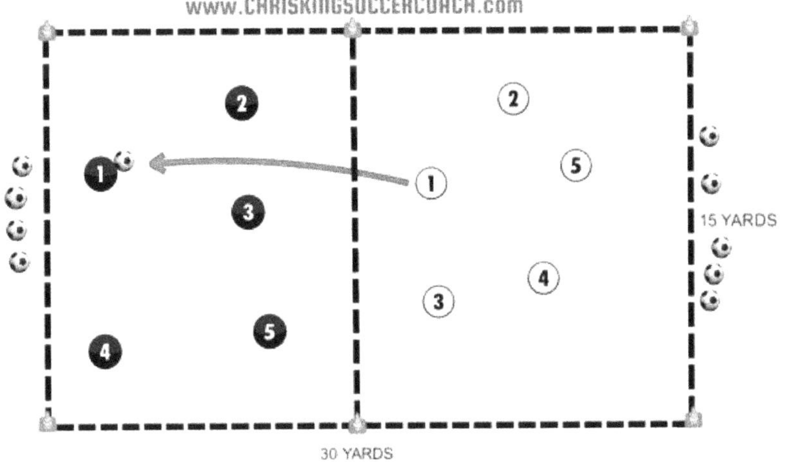

In Play: Blacks have made 3 passes so now another White team mate (White #3) can go across and help with the press.

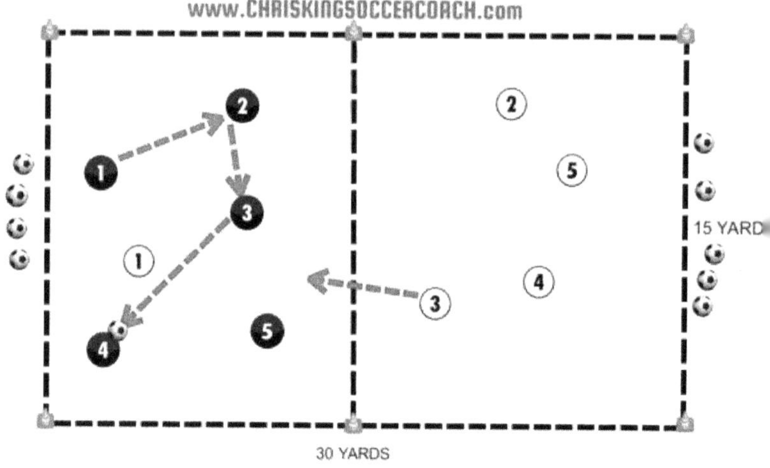

CHAPTER 4
SESSION 1 DRILL 2:
OVERLOADING AREAS TO PLAY FORWARD

PURPOSE:

- Overload the midfield and support the forward player when the ball goes forward.

SET UP:

- 11 Players (alternatively 9 or 13 players - add 2 more in zone B, or for 9 players remove the two outside players)
- 4 Cones + 4 discs
- 15x30 yard area
- 20 minutes

THE DRILL:

- In Zones A & C, it is 1v1 with both Blacks and White locked in their zones.
- In Zone B, it is 2v2+3 (when in possession it becomes 5v2 with the two outside #5 players and middle player #6.
- The 2 #5 outside players may move along the line in Zone B and are on the side of the team in possession.
- When in possession, one of the midfielders in Zone B (Blacks in this case) must move into the other zones (Zones A & C) creating a 2v1 situation. This makes the players support the striker and move forward with the pass.

• The purpose of the game is to move the ball from one target player at one end to the other at the other end, keeping good possession of the ball. For example, once Black #1 in Zone A has gained possession and a player from his team has entered Zone A to support (even if that player doesn't get used), the Blacks try and move it to through Zone B to Black #4 in Zone C.

• If the defenders (White) win the ball, they try to move it from end to end the same as the Blacks.

KEY POINTS:

- Patience in possession.
- Use depth, width and length.
- Expose the overload by using the spare players.

COACHES NOTES:

• Continuous play, swap overload players (#5's & #6) every few minutes.

• Have spare balls spread around the outside for continuous, quick play.

• Make sure an extra attacking player is getting into Zone A or C quickly to support the attacking player as this is what you would want in a match.

• Quick forward passing where possible but also be patient and keep possession if required.

• If a player gives away possession too much from being lazy make them do 5 push ups quickly.

CHANGES/PROGRESSION:

• You can remove the 2 outside players if there are not enough numbers.

• Once play is flowing well and the players are engaged, make it so that if one team goes from Zone A to Zone C and back twice, the opposition do 10 push ups. This keeps the intensity up.

Starting shape: 1v1 in Zones A & C. 2v2 plus 3 overload players playing with the team in possession in Zone B.

(Image: Session 1 - drill 2 - A)

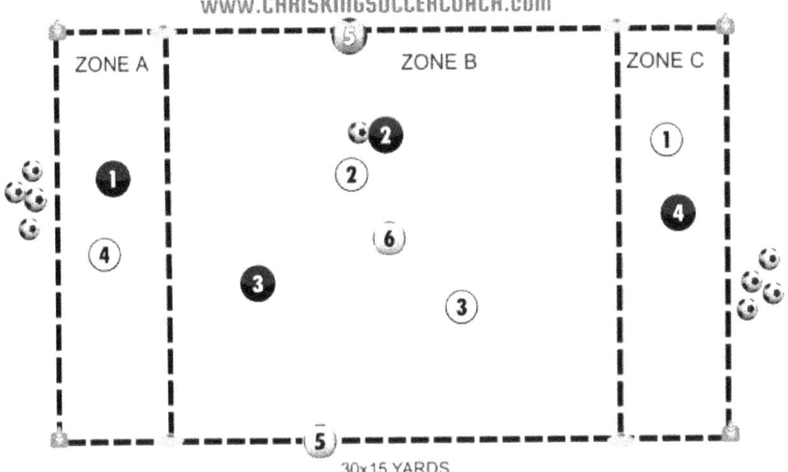

In play: When Black #2 passes into Black #1, Black #3 should enter Zone A to support. Once this is achieved, the Blacks try & move it back through the midfield (Zone B) and into Black #4 in Zone C. Always get an extra player in to support the players in Zone A & C before the ball can be played back out.

(Image: Session 1 - drill 2 - B)

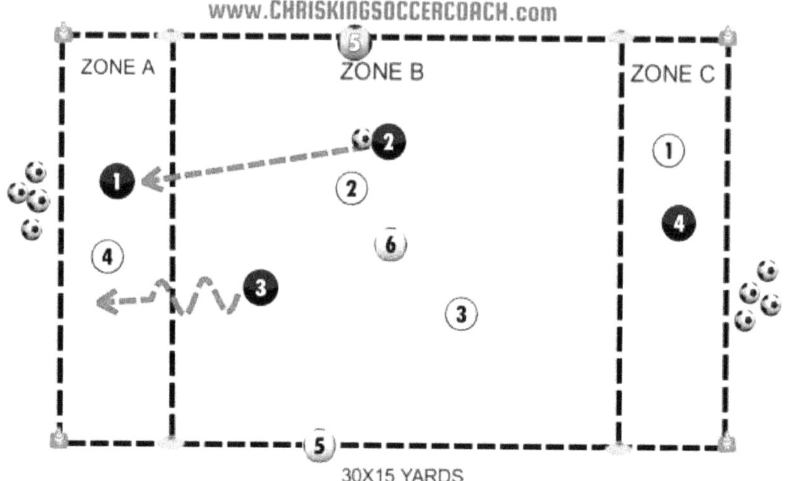

In play 2: In this example, Black #1 has received it and Black #3 has come in to support. Black #1 passes to Black #3 who passes back out to the overload player (#6) who uses the outside overload player (#5) who bounces it into Black #2 as they work it from one end to the other. (Image: Session 1 - drill 2 - C)

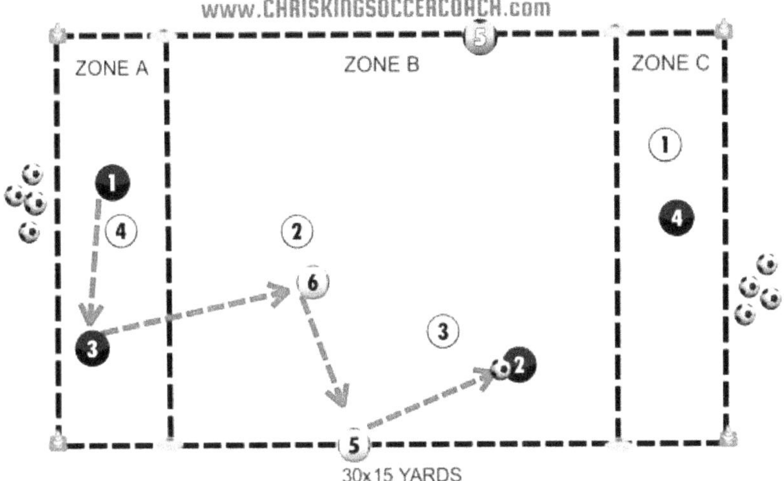

CHAPTER 5

SESSION 1 DRILL 3: COMBINATION PLAY TO SCORE GOALS

(SMALL SIDED GAME)

PURPOSE:

- Overload the attacking areas to get intense, repetitive, quick fire shots on goals to give practice to both attacking players and goalkeepers.

SET UP:

- 11 Players (2 GK if available) (alternatively 9 or up to 14. Add or remove players as needed and adjust the size of the area accordingly.)
- 7 Cones
- 2 x medium goals (small or large if no medium)
- 25x40 yard area
- 20 minutes

THE DRILL:

- 2 teams of 4 with 3 Whites in one half v 1 Black, and 3 Blacks in the opposite half v 1 White.
- Overload player (#5) can play anywhere on the pitch with the team in possession.
- Teams look to combine from the GK in a 3+1v1 to shoot from within their own half. The player in the attacking half follows up for rebounds.
- If a goal is scored, that team keeps possession and play starts from their GK. If the shot is missed the opposition GK starts play.

KEY POINTS:

- Use depth, width and length.
- Expose the overload & use the spare player.

COACHES NOTES:

- Tell the GK's to be aware to start play quickly once a ball goes out (ie if a shot is missed the GK from that end quickly starts play. This encourages players to get in position quickly and to take advantage of other players who may have switched off).

- Have spare balls behind each goal.

- Push the players to do everything at pace.

- It will seem heavily overloaded (4v1+GK) to the team in possession when playing out but it is meant to be so the intensity is kept up and lots of shots are taken).

CHANGES:

- Challenge players individually (ie do things at pace; with 2 touches; move the ball to one side and shoot early).

- Limit touches to one or two.

PROGRESSION:

- The team in possession can play to their team mate in the attacking half to finish. Also, one player may dribble or pass across to the other half to shoot or combine with the attacking team mate in the attacking half.

Starting Shape: White attacking to the left, Blacks to the right.

3 defenders v 1 attacker in each half with an overload player (#5) playing with the team in possession. Play starts from the goalkeepers (or a coach from the outside if no goalies), if a team scores they keep possession and their goalkeeper restarts instantly. (Image: Session 1 - drill 3 - A)

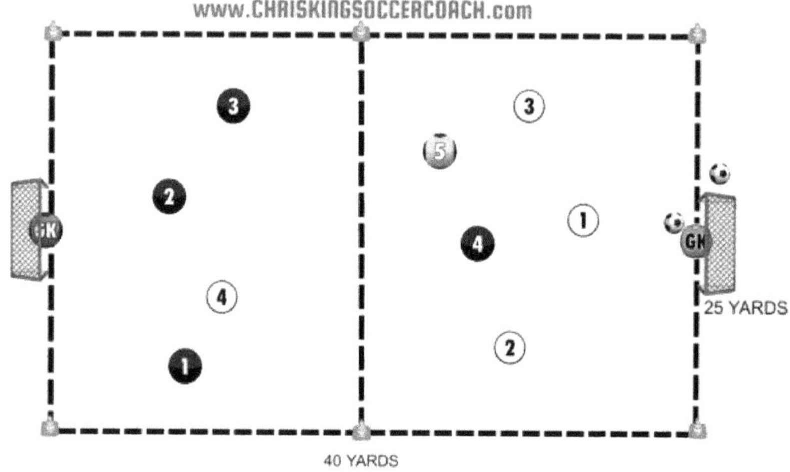

In Play: The player in possession (in this case #5) shoots & White #4 follows in for any rebounds. If there is a goal scored White keep possession & start from their GK again. (Image: Session 1 - drill 3 - B)

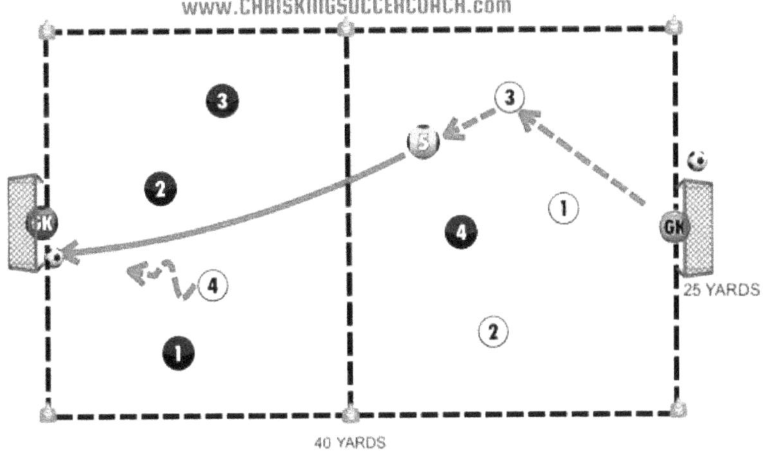

Progression: The player in possession (in this case #5) can either dribble into the other half and shoot, or pass to the forward (White #4) and enter that half and support them. This improves the players' decision making. (Image: Session 1 - drill 3 - C)

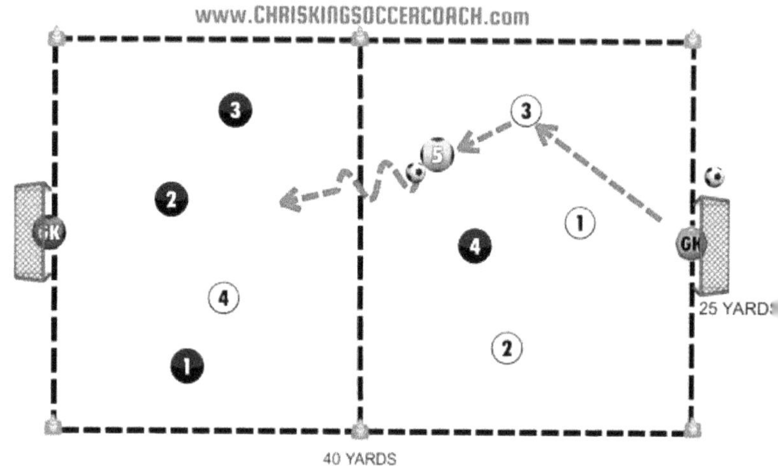

From “Attacking & Shooting Drills For Soccer Coaches”

CHAPTER 2

DRILL 2 - RAPID ATTACKING

PURPOSE:

- The attacking teams put intense pressure on the defending team and get shots on goal without overplaying it.

SET UP:

- 15 Players + 2 Goalkeepers (alternatively 11 to 12 players)
- Half a pitch

THE DRILL:

- Pitch is divided into 3 sections with the middle third a 15-20 yard channel.

- 3 teams of 5 (or alternatively 3 teams of 4, or you can have less players defending ie 4v3v4).

- Defenders start in the middle channel.

- The attacking teams start behind each goal, alternating turns to attack. Balls in each goal.

- Defenders ARE NOT allowed in the third where the attackers start. They must wait for the attackers to enter the middle third and then can tackle/defend.

- Attackers try to get through the middle third and shoot on goal - they can shoot from the middle third or attacking third.

- A maximum of 3 players from the attackers and 2 defenders can enter the furthest third.

- If the defenders win the ball they have 15-20 seconds to score at the opposite end and can go wherever they want.

- Once there is a shot or ball goes out of play, the attacking team runs off back to their goal, defenders reset back in the middle section and the other attacking team starts from the other end.

- Play goes for 2 or 3 run throughs from both ends and then swap the middle defensive team.

KEY POINTS:

- High intensity - as soon as there is a shot get the attackers off and defenders reset and let the other attacking team start almost straight away.

- Get the players from the attacking team that aren't on the ball to do overlapping runs and cross field movement.

COACHES NOTES:

- Are the attacking team organised and moving the ball from side to side to disorganise the defence?

- Are the goalkeepers organising and talking to the teams (goalkeeper talk is a vital part of defensive play and can also start an attacking movement)?

- Encourage the attackers to follow in on their shot in case the goalkeeper fumbles or if it is parried back into the box.

CHANGES/PROGRESSION:

- Which team can score the most goals? Add up at the end and give punishment to the other two teams.

Starting Shape: 5 players at each end with 5 in the defensive middle third. A goalkeeper in each goal.

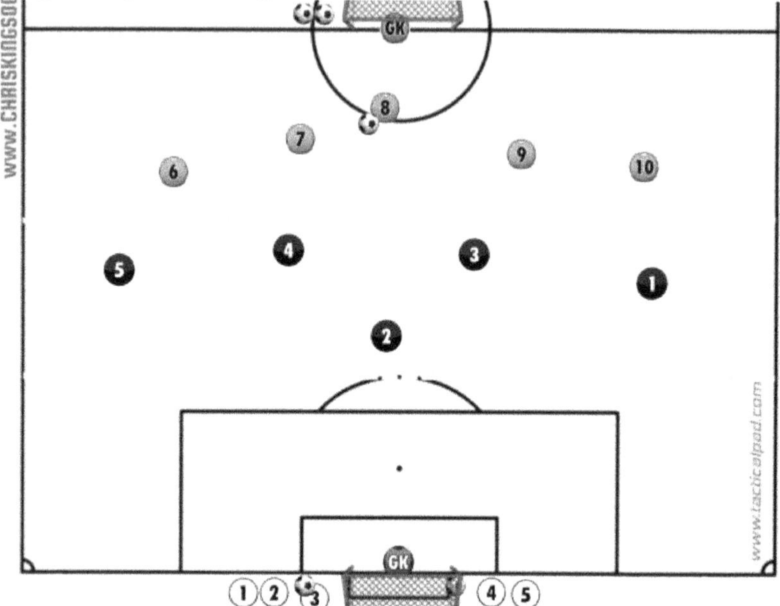

In Play 1: The attacking team moves into the middle third. Black defensive team can now shut players down and tackle.

In Play 2: The attacking team passes the ball quickly to get the defensive team out of shape. #8 passes to #6 and passes through to #7.

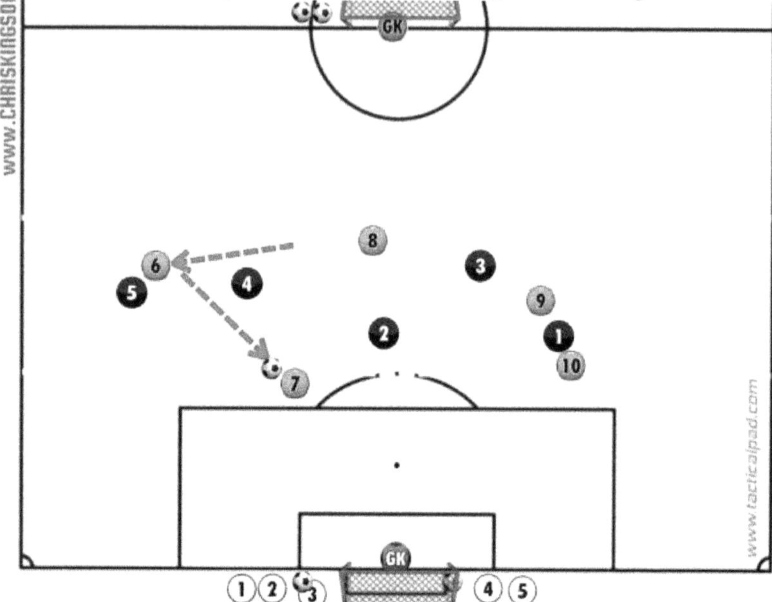

In Play 3: #7 has a first time shot as #10 looks to follow the shot in.

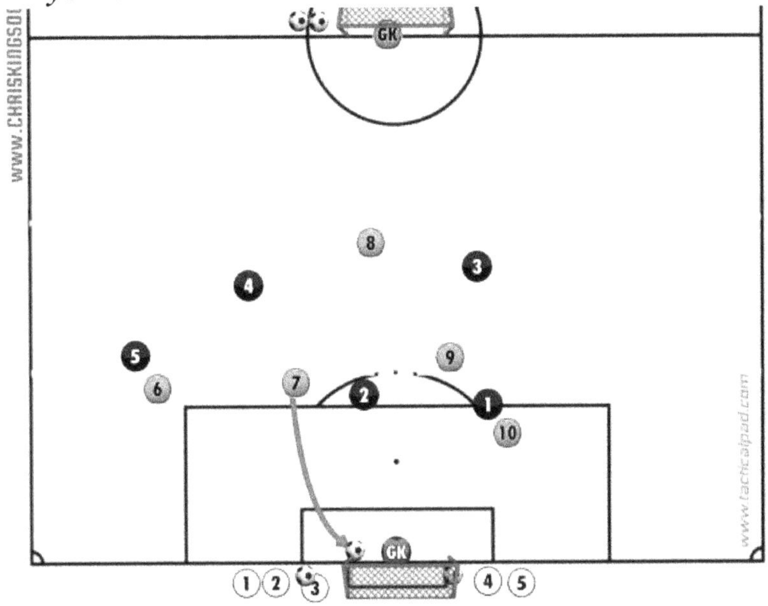

In Play 4: The shot goes in so the attacking team runs back to their end and the defensive team returns to the middle third.

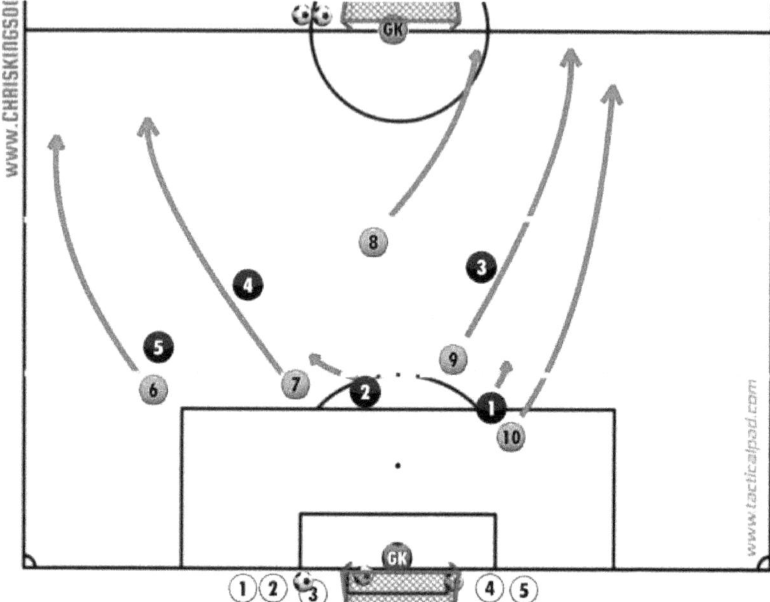

In Play 5: The other attacking team (White) starts their attack.

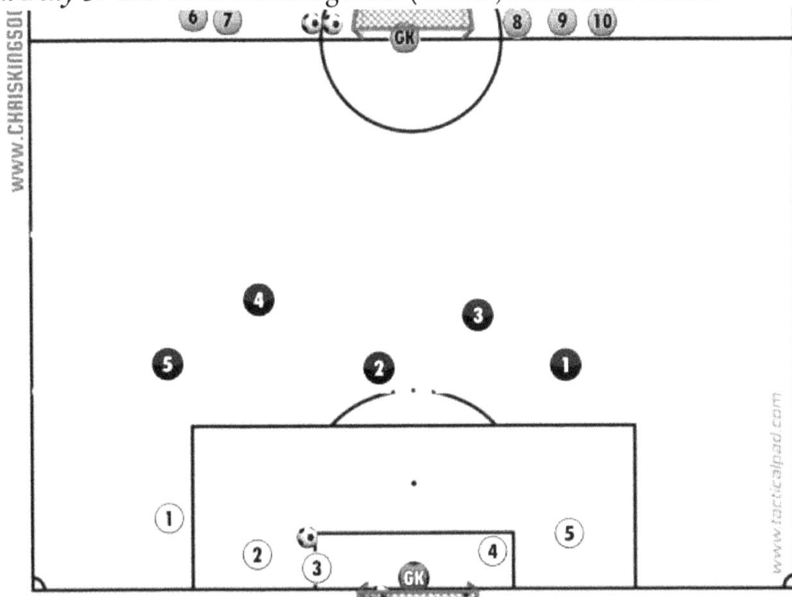

In Play 6: In this image the attacking team lost possession so the defensive team had 15-20 seconds to score at the other end. Black #2 slots it away nicely.

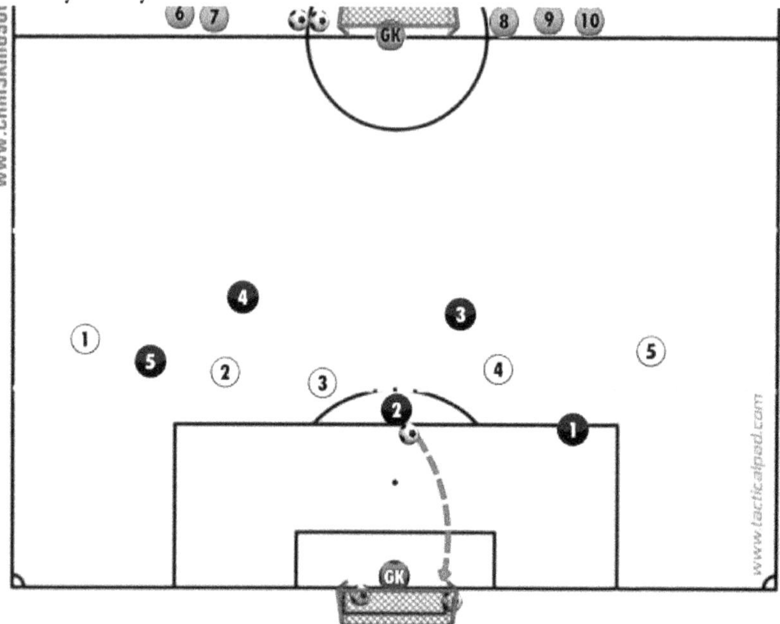

Don't miss out!

Visit the website below and you can sign up to receive emails whenever Chris King publishes a new book. There's no charge and no obligation.

https://books2read.com/r/B-A-QGPU-ZCHIC

BOOKS 2 READ

Connecting independent readers to independent writers.

www.ingramcontent.com/pod-product-compliance
Ingram Content Group UK Ltd.
Pitfield, Milton Keynes, MK11 3LW, UK
UKHW021655190726
13853UKWH00001B/284

9 798223 408529